LIVE
HAPPY

LIVE
HAPPY

100 Simple Ways
to Fill Your Life with Joy

Bridget Grenville-Cleave and Ilona Boniwell

m

CONTENTS

INTRODUCTION

Today's world can be complex and stressful for many people. This book can help you look at your own behaviour, thoughts and feelings objectively and change the things that negatively affect your happiness. Some of the information in this book may seem very much like common sense, while some may seem surprising or counterintuitive. What is important is to take each item to heart and put it into practice.

There is a genetic component involved that scientists say is responsible for many people feeling unhappy or depressed, but genetic make-up is not the only factor that affects mood. Your habits, your relationships, your environment, and especially what you think about them, have a huge impact. It's important to acknowledge that no one can be happy all the time. Everyone will experience some sadness, disappointment or other negative emotion at some point in their lives. This is part of what it means to be human, and without negative emotions you wouldn't be able to appreciate positive emotions.

You can improve every area of your happiness: your relationship with yourself and with others, your work life, your home life and even your health. As we get older, many of us stick with old habits, some of which can be unhelpful; this book is designed to offer you new ideas about the little things you can do that will make a difference. As you discover the factors in this book that are most effective for you, make a little note about the best ones. In applying them to your own life, take some time to congratulate yourself; the more you understand that increasing your happiness is working, the more motivated you will be and the happier you can become.

This book presents the factors that most influence human wellbeing and happiness, either positively or negatively. The information is based on thorough academic research, with information gathered from over 100 different journal articles, books and reports. All of this research points to how different aspects of life affect our level of happiness and what you can do to change them. Of course, people are individuals with their own wants and needs: what works for me isn't necessarily the same for you. Science shows us, however, that there are some aspects of happiness that are pretty widespread, so most of the factors in this book will be relevant to your own life.

Many positive psychologists agree that the factor that most influences your level of wellbeing is your genes, which you cannot change. That said, just because your happiness baseline is for the most part genetically determined does not mean that you cannot become happier. What the diagram below shows us is that, while

Happiness is made up as follows:

LIFE CIRCUMSTANCES
INTENTIONAL ACTIVITY
GENES

10%   40%   50%

50 per cent of your happiness is iinfluenced by your genes, 10 per cent is influenced by life circumstances, such as age, gender, social class and the community you live in. They make only a small difference to your level of happiness, and probably not as much as you might think. Even so, there are ways you can become happier regardless of your circumstance.

The remaining 40 per cent of the diagram shows us that a large portion of your happiness is completely within your control. The advice in this book focuses largely on daily activities and emotions that influence your happiness and what you can change about them. These are the areas of your life where you can really make a conscious effort to improve your happiness.

What is happiness?

A large part of our happiness is made up of our emotional wellbeing – not just whether we feel positive or negative today, but whether or not in general we tend to be resilient, curious, optimistic or simply thankful for the good things that happen in our lives. Often we attribute our emotional wellbeing to our genes or our personality, so it's tempting to conclude that there is nothing to be done. The problem then is that we think we cannot influence it in any way, whereas given the time, knowledge and motivation, it is perfectly possible to change your emotional wellbeing for the better. So if you tend to be a bit grumpy, the good news is that there's no reason to stay that way!

Happiness isn't just about emotional wellbeing; physical wellbeing has a significant part to play, too. It's not all about how physically healthy you are either. How healthy you think you are is what really counts (see page 16).

Your relationships with other people will also contribute significantly to how you feel every day. Even the briefest of encounters with acquaintances or complete strangers are opportunities to boost your happiness, and theirs. No grand gestures: just taking the time to smile, say hello, be polite and be helpful is all that's needed. What really matters is the quality of our relationships with others, and don't forget that sometimes people we think of as friends may subconsciously be doing us more harm than good. So think about the important relationships you have, how they add to your overall wellbeing and ways in which you can improve them further. In terms of increasing your happiness, time spent doing this will be a very good investment.

Happiness is also about positive achievement and meaning, in other words, fulfilment. It's not easy to say how crucial fulfilment is overall since it depends on each individual. Where science can help is by indicating if certain types of activity are likely to lead to longer-lasting happiness. By and large, the more hedonistic happiness associated with physical activities like eating, drinking or shopping bring short-term pleasure, but can work against your happiness in the long-term. So concentrate on the things you can do and the choices you can make to achieve enduring happiness. There are a whole range of activities you can do to help increase your overall wellbeing and happiness.

A word of caution: everyone is an individual and it is impossible to predict with 100 per cent certainty how happy or not you'll be if you participate in the various activities. This book should be seen as a way of getting you to think about what you can do differently to boost your happiness. And if you have real concerns about either your mental or physical wellbeing, consult your doctor, therapist or a counsellor immediately.

BE HAPPY NOW

What would you do if you won the lottery? You'd be happier of course, right? Well, actually, no, not necessarily. The reason, say scientists, is something called the 'adaptation effect'.

Adaptation works in two ways. Say you did win the lottery – in the short term the simple things that you previously enjoyed, for instance drinking a cool beer on a hot summer's day, would seem less satisfying in comparison with the new pleasures that the money brings you.

In the long term the novelty of the good fortune wears off, as it is bound to do. So, while you might imagine that winning £1 million would be the answer to all of your prayers, science tells us that, actually, you will just get used to the new pleasures that the extra money brings you. One small glimmer of hope, however, is that winning a moderate amount on the lottery may reduce your psychological stress one to two years later!

WHILE YOU MIGHT IMAGINE THAT WINNING THE LOTTERY WOULD MAKE YOU HAPPIER, SCIENCE TELLS US YOU WILL JUST GET USED TO THE NEW PLEASURES THAT THE EXTRA MONEY BRINGS YOU.

Studies on people who have suffered a terrible misfortune, such as a paralysing accident, show that the adaptation effect also works for them. Typically they come to terms with the negative event and do not appear nearly as unhappy as you might expect.

If happy events don't improve happiness in the long run, there are two factors that come into play. Firstly, we should learn how to be happy in the moment, even though (or more so that) it is fleeting. Secondly, we can learn to be happy with what we have right now; remember the simple things that you enjoyed previously.

STAY HAPPY

2

GET BETTER WITH AGE

We're remarkably bad at remembering accurately how happy we were in the past and predicting how happy we'll be in the future. We expect to be happier when we're in a romantic relationship, when we're promoted or when we lose weight. As it happens, these events only boost our happiness level temporarily, but then it returns pretty quickly to what it was before.

The same thing happens with negative events. Most people adjust to their circumstances over time and are only marginally less happy, if at all. This inability to predict our happiness accurately might be one of the reasons why we're afraid of getting older – we expect to be less happy.

In fact, happiness has more to do with the process of ageing. Typically, happiness levels start high, then decline, reaching a low point around the mid-40s, and then increase again. This may be because, as we mature, we reprioritize, redirecting our energies away from things we can't do towards things we can, focusing on more meaningful social and emotional goals rather than on material acquisition. So don't worry that you'll be a grumpy senior citizen; in all likelihood you'll be happier than you were in your 40s.

3

EMBRACE YOUR EMOTIONS

In recent years, we've been encouraged to acknowledge and celebrate the differences between the sexes, recognizing that both have unique strengths (and weaknesses). When it comes to happiness, it seems that men and women are roughly equally happy in nearly every country, suggesting that gender per se has little effect on happiness.

There is evidence that women's overall wellbeing is more influenced by events that happened in the past, while men's is more influenced by recent events. Not only that but women, on the whole, show more intense positive emotion than men, as well as more negative emotion, typically depression. Put another way, women are both happier and unhappier than men! Whether male or female, we should learn to accept and celebrate these differences.

· ·

WOMEN'S OVERALL WELLBEING IS MORE INFLUENCED BY EVENTS IN THE PAST, WHILE MEN'S IS MORE INFLUENCED BY RECENT EVENTS.

· ·

4

APPRECIATE WHAT YOU HAVE

Does having more money actually make you happier? When comparing different countries' happiness in relation to wealth, it appears that the level of happiness rises as wealth increases. However, other factors may contribute to this wealth–happiness link. Richer industrially developed countries also tend to be more democratic than poorer less developed ones, for example.

> **IT IS NOT THE MAN WHO HAS TOO LITTLE, BUT THE MAN WHO CRAVES MORE, WHO IS POOR.**
>
> SENECA

Wealthier people seem to be a little happier than the rest of us but not as much as you might think. The average annual income in developed countries has been growing steadily since the end of World War II, but happiness levels have not risen at the same rate.

The reason for this seems to be that people care more about their relative income than they do about their absolute income; it's down to your perception of your own wealth in relation to others'. Try to visualize your situation against the bigger picture and you may find that you appreciate what you already have.

COMPARISON OF WEALTH AND HAPPINESS BY COUNTRY

Country	GDP per capita (£)	% satisfied with life
USA	29,300	65
Canada	24,300	71
GB	22,500	59
Germany	22,000	48
France	21,500	57
Poland	10,300	39
Peru	4,800	41
India	1,700	41
Kenya	1,000	16
Uganda	700	7

THINK YOURSELF HEALTHY

The immune systems of happy people are more effective than those of people who are not. Positive emotions increase pain tolerance and can even protect us against death from alcohol-related liver disease and heart disease, even after adjusting for factors such as age, gender, exercise, alcohol consumption and smoking.

So does good physical health make you happier? In fact, your physical health makes very little difference to happiness, unless you are severely disabled. What matters more is whether or not you think you're healthy!

What you think about your health is influenced more by your personality (see entry 21) and coping strategies than by your objective health.

PERCEPTIONS OF HEALTH ARE MORE IMPORTANT TO HAPPINESS THAN ACTUAL HEALTH.

So perceptions of health are more important to happiness than actual health. If you have the misfortune to be ill, find ways to think differently about your situation, such as reframing important life goals or comparing yourself to others who are worse off.

EAT YOURSELF HEALTHY

What you eat can effect both your physical and psychological health. Eating too many saturated fats and trans fatty acids increases the risk of heart disease, obesity, and type 2 diabetes, and a diet lacking essential vitamins, minerals and omega-3s can lead to depression, anxiety, poor concentration, mood swings and fatigue as well as increased aggression. So ensure you eat a healthy diet, avoiding the foods below.

Foods to avoid

- Processed foods such as bread and ready meals.
- Saturated fats found in dairy products, as well as palm oil and coconut oil.
- Alcohol – most adults can drink alcohol in moderation without any problem (see page 71), but it easily decreases your self-control and impairs your judgement, making risky behaviour much more attractive.
- Refined foods such as white sugar, rice and flour.
- Caffeine – it stimulates the central nervous system and boosts energy levels, making you feel more alert, but you can develop a tolerance to it quickly, which means you'd need to drink more and more in order to get the same effect.

EAT YOURSELF HAPPY

A balanced diet with the right combination of vitamins and minerals plays a vital role in mental wellbeing. Getting enough vitamins and minerals is essential to balance your mood. Keep yourself fit, healthy and happy on a diet that draws on a balance of all five food groups (starchy carbohydrates; fruit and vegetables; dairy; meat and fish; fat and sugar).

Vitamins and minerals to boost your mood

- **Folic Acid** (from broccoli, asparagus and peas) helps tackle fatigue, confusion and irritability.
- **Vitamin B12** (from meat, salmon, milk, eggs and yeast extract). Severe deficiency results in loss of memory, mental dysfunction and depression.
- **Vitamin C** (from peppers, broccoli, oranges and kiwi fruit). High-dose vitamin C supplements have been shown to reduce depression.
- **Selenium** (from brazil nuts, bread, fish, meat and eggs) for improved mood.
- **Iron** (from liver, dried fruit, whole grains and dark-green leafy vegetables). Helps avoid fatigue, irritability and apathy and improve concentration.
- **Zinc** (from meat, shellfish, dairy and cereal products). Depression is a common symptom of zinc deficiency.
- **Omega-3** (fatty fish, eggs, nuts and seeds). Deficiency is thought to be responsible for increased incidences of depression and anxiety.

FEEL BEAUTIFUL

Many people put a high value on appearance. But for all that, does your appearance actually make you happier? There is recent research to suggest that Botox can be used to treat depression, by removing the participants' ability to frown, but spending thousands of pounds on permanent plastic surgery may only make you feel better in the short run.

Most people would agree that taking care of your appearance provides an important boost to your self-respect. Clearly there are acknowledged benefits to being more beautiful, which may result in your feeling better. It's interesting, however, that happy people tend to believe they're more beautiful, regardless of what other people think. So, whether it's the fact they're happy that helps them feel beautiful or feeling beautiful that makes them happier, it's how you feel on the inside that counts here.

HAPPY PEOPLE TEND TO BELIEVE THEY'RE MORE BEAUTIFUL, REGARDLESS OF WHAT OTHER PEOPLE THINK.

9

IMPROVE YOUR MENTAL WELLBEING

Research has shown that psychological wellbeing is not merely the absence of negative emotions; it also requires positive emotions, which is what positive psychologists study. Positive mental activities – for example, writing a gratitude diary – have been shown to improve psychological wellbeing, actually increasing happiness levels. Try some of the suggestions below.

How to improve your mental wellbeing

- Start every day with meditation (see page 93).
- Do regular physical exercise (see page 72).
- Write a gratitude diary.
- Keep a house plant (see page 32).
- Have a good laugh at least once a day (see page 78).
- Smile at and/or say hello to a stranger at least once a day.
- Do a good deed for someone every day – it doesn't have to be elaborate (see page 85).
- Lose yourself in a favourite activity, whether it's fly-fishing, stamp-collecting or learning a foreign language (see page 64).

10

ENGAGE WITH THE WORLD

HI!

According to positive psychologists, personality is one of the strongest predictors of subjective wellbeing, and two specific personality traits, extroversion (how talkative, energetic and assertive you are) and neuroticism (how tense, moody and anxious you are), can predict how happy you will be in 10 years' time. If you're high on the extroversion dimension and low on the neuroticism dimension, you're likely to be pretty happy.

That's not to say that you can't be happy if you don't have these personality traits. Just as famous personalities can be manufactured, so can you develop a more extroverted personality. Try adopting extrovert behaviours such as assertiveness and engaging with others, and work towards reducing your anxiety (see page 58).

FIND YOUR FLOW

'Flow' occurs when you're so fully absorbed in what you're doing that you don't notice what's going on around you. You often lose track of time, and afterwards you feel great. Athletes call it 'being in the zone'.

Flow is a tried and tested pathway to achieving greater happiness, through controlling your inner experience or consciousness. In order to be able to get into a flow state with your favourite activity, the levels of challenge and skill need to be in equilibrium. Make sure the activity has clear goals and that you get direct feedback about what you are doing well or not so well so that you can change what you do as needed.

What works for you may be different to what works for others, so try different activities until you find something where it's easy to lose track of time and you don't get caught up in your thoughts and concerns. Once you have found that activity, develop it and challenge yourself. The more you get into flow, the happier you'll feel!

GET RID OF CLUTTER

Clutter is contagious, oppressive and stubborn. It accumulates on our desks and in our homes and it's often difficult to shift. But kicking the clutter habit can bring high rewards in increased productivity, improved self-esteem and lower stress levels.

THE PRESENCE OF EXCESS STUFF SENDS SUBCONSCIOUS SIGNALS THAT YOU DON'T HAVE YOUR LIFE UNDER CONTROL.

Neuroscientists at Princeton University assessed the effect of an organized versus disorganized environment on people's task performance. The results showed that we are distracted by surrounding mess, leading to decreased attention span and poorer performance.

In a separate study, a link was found between high levels of the stress hormone cortisol and a high density of household objects. This may be because the presence of excess stuff sends subconscious signals to yourself that you don't have your life under control, with an effect on self-esteem. So set aside some time each week to be ruthless with your possessions: ditch any junk.

13

INDEPENDENCE FROM MONEY

In one analysis of 286 empirical studies involving over 150,000 participants across the globe, psychologists Pinquart and Sörensen have shown that higher social class is linked to three measures of wellbeing: life satisfaction, self-esteem and happiness.

YOU'RE LIKELY TO BE HAPPIER AND HEALTHIER THE MORE YOU FEEL THAT YOU CAN DIRECT THE COURSE OF YOUR LIFE.

That may not come as a surprise, but the reason why people of a higher social class enjoy their lives more isn't actually because they earn more money. Psychologists like Daniel Nettle have thought that, rather than money, it's the amount of personal control you have that contributes to wellbeing, life satisfaction and health.

So, you're likely to be happier and healthier the more you feel that you can direct the course of your life and manage your health, work, family and relationships successfully. Though you may not be able to change your social class or the money you bring home, you can work on taking control of your finances to develop autonomy. If it's this, rather than money, that brings happiness, maybe we should encourage children to develop a strong sense of personal control, rather than find a career that will simply make them rich.

GET SOME SUN

When the sun shines, you may find you're more cheerful, more able to deal with life's little problems, and you notice that other people are more helpful and smile more, too. Sunshine has well-known health benefits: the human body uses sunlight to create vitamin D, which protects against many ageing-related diseases, such as heart disease, cancer and rheumatoid arthritis. Plus, it's long been established that sunshine (specifically bright light, rather than warmth) improves mood, by raising the level of serotonin produced by the brain.

While sunshine can boost your mood, be aware that over time you will acclimatize and return to your 'normal' happiness baseline (see page 7). Luckily, the same applies to unfavourable weather conditions: bad weather won't make you miserable for life. So, even if sunshine cannot permanently make you happier, it can certainly give you a temporary lift.

15

SAY 'HI' TO YOUR NEIGHBOURS

Social relationships are fundamental to human evolution; we wouldn't have survived as a species without the ability to live and work in groups, giving each other support in times of need and sharing in times of plenty. Because of this, the community you live in plays a vital role in your happiness.

The quality of a community tends to be measured in terms of its cohesiveness, which is determined by a combination of similar factors such as trust, reciprocity, mutual help and volunteering. Though, as you can imagine, this can be difficult to measure! The World Values Survey provides much-needed insights into the quality of communities by country. It includes questions about trust as well as asking about the volunteer work that respondents do.

The results fluctuate between years, but it is interesting to note that very few countries indicate a majority when it comes to trust – even in the more trusting communities many consider it wise to be cautious before imparting their trust. One way to build trust in your community is to increase communication and develop friendships locally.

According to John Helliwell, Professor Emeritus of Economics at the University of British Columbia, who has analysed 20 years' worth of World Values Survey data, the differences in national average trust have a large and significant effect on reported happiness, and an increase in national trust levels would lead to an increase in subjective wellbeing. This is both a remarkable and exciting discovery. By finding ways to build more trust in society, between the young and the old, for example, or between different ethnic groups, we can increase our happiness at the same time.

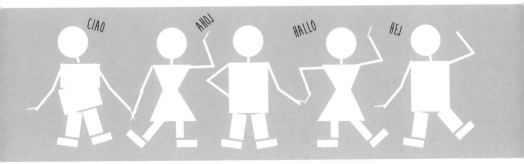

IMPROVE YOUR LUCK

Psychologist Professor Richard Wiseman of Hertfordshire University has studied luck for well over a decade and believes that, the lottery apart, luck isn't a purely random phenomenon, nor is it caused by psychic powers or intelligence. Instead, it comes from your beliefs, and your behaviours connected to them.

BELIEVING IN GOOD LUCK CAN LEAD TO FEELINGS OF OPTIMISM, WHICH IN TURNS LEADS TO GREATER MENTAL WELLBEING.

Rather than regarding luck as an uncontrollable external factor that doesn't influence our feelings of wellbeing, psychologists are now speculating that believing in good luck might lead to feelings of optimism, which in turn lead to greater mental wellbeing. In other words, according to Wiseman, how you behave can influence how lucky you are. In fact, Wiseman has four simple steps for changing bad luck into good (see below).

How to improve your luck

- Maximize your opportunities.
- Listen to your intuition.
- Expect good luck in the future.
- Look on the positive side of bad luck.

CHANGE YOUR REACTION

Some people have the capacity to turn the most terrible tragedy around, overcoming extreme hardship, poverty, violence or torture, as they react by actually improving relationships, achieving a greater appreciation for life and a greater sense of personal strength as they do so. In spite of, or more accurately, because of, the trauma suffered, they grow and develop as human beings. This phenomenon is called post-traumatic growth.

The process of post-traumatic growth relies on making sense of the trauma and then assimilating it into a new view of life. Imagine a beautiful vase that smashes into a hundred tiny pieces. Recreating the vase by gluing the pieces back together will leave it looking nearly the same, but it won't be anywhere near as strong as it was before. Post-traumatic growth is more like creating an entirely new object from the pieces, not a vase, but something equally beautiful, like a mosaic. While tragedy and trauma are obviously not beneficial to our happiness, they can lead to greater physical and psychological health afterwards.

LET THE POSITIVE OUTWEIGH THE NEGATIVE

You can be simultaneously happy in one area of your life (for example, your relationship) and unhappy in another (for example, your work). Different cultures have different approaches to happiness, emphasising different goals and values.

In individualistic Western countries, happiness is often seen as a reflection of personal achievement: whether you have made the most of your life. In the more collectivist nations such as Japan and South Korea, people have a more fatalistic attitude towards happiness. These different attitudes affect how people subjectively report happiness and satisfaction in life. What's more, the things that give people happiness, satisfaction and meaning in their lives vary considerably between cultures.

It's no surprise then that when we consider the relationship between ethnicity and happiness, differences do start to emerge, not so much to do with actual levels of wellbeing and life satisfaction, but with how we're brought up to achieve them. We can learn from these different cultures to decide what we use to determine our own happiness.

How different cultures report happiness and satisfaction

- Among young Koreans, satisfaction with school contributes more to their overall wellbeing.

- For young people in the United States, focusing on one's own goals and independence are more strongly associated with their life satisfaction.

- Japanese workers report much more satisfaction with their work than American workers. This is thought to be due to the fact that the concept of work is more meaningful for the Japanese than for Americans.

- Asian Americans, Koreans and the Japanese pay more attention to positive daily events than do European Americans.

CONNECT WITH NATURE

TURN OVER A NEW LEAF

It's clear that your physical surroundings can have a significant impact on how you feel, but does contact with nature make you happier? Research shows that people living in environments that lack natural spaces have higher levels of aggression than those living in greener environments. Natural spaces do reduce the mental fatigue caused by tasks that require profound concentration, and views of greenery have a positive effect on physical health, reducing blood pressure and stress.

The reasons why this happens are not entirely clear. It may be that we're particularly drawn to landscapes featuring plants, flowers and water because they contributed to our survival and reproduction as early humans. Whatever the explanation, there's no doubt that natural environments can make us feel both mentally and physically healthier. So, visit a park or the countryside at the weekend, spend time in the garden or buy houseplants if you don't have a garden.

EXPERIENCE JOY

FEEL UPLIFTED

Psychologist Barbara Fredrickson has suggested that positive emotions expand our attention rather than focusing it (as negative emotions do). So, experiencing joy leads us to want to play and be creative, feeling interested leads us to explore and experience, and feeling contented leads us to savour and appreciate.

The second purpose of positive emotions is that they 'undo' the effect of negative emotions and enhance resilience and the ability to cope. Humour increases pain tolerance for example. Resilient people experience more positive emotions after a negative event (see page 45), which leads them to feel increased optimism, wellbeing and tranquility as well as protecting them against depression.

REALIZE YOUR POTENTIAL

Confidence impacts how much we persist in the face of difficulties and affects how we feel about ourselves; it can make us more or less vulnerable to stress and depression; and it affects the immune system and activates endorphins, our natural pain killers. It's perfectly possible to be self-assured in some parts of your life, and not in others.

To build confidence, be specific about the when, where and how you lack confidence. Then, work to improve that. Don't allow a lack of confidence in a specific area spread to other things.

Self-confidence is a set of beliefs about yourself, not an inherent skill or personality trait. You can be very competent and capable, and still feel a lack of self-confidence. It is very possible to change your confidence level, and it does not have to determine your behaviour. Some psychologists believe that confidence, along with persistence and effort, is a more powerful determinant of your success than actual innate ability.

One of the most effective ways to build confidence is by actually trying to do the thing in which you lack confidence. Expect to feel uncomfortable at first, but welcome it, because it's a sign that you're learning something new. So, confidence, or the lack of it, isn't fixed, which is good news – it means that we can learn how to become more confident.

How to build your confidence

- Identify those areas of your life in which you would like to have more confidence.

- Be specific about what it is that you want to achieve by improving your confidence.

- Break your goal down into small steps so that you can build your confidence gradually, rather than jumping straight in.

- Seek support from someone close to you; tell them what you are going to do so that they can encourage you to have more faith in yourself and help you to make bolder choices.

- Don't worry about feeling uncomfortable – it's natural to feel awkward as you step outside of your normal comfort zone. Be brave and persevere with your goals.

22

TAKE CONTROL OF YOUR DECISIONS

It is not salary or conditions that determine how happy people are at work, nor even whether or not their job is a vocation (see page 114). Experts have suggested that the difference between those jobs that give the most satisfaction and those that give the least is due to whether or not the employee feels in control of what they do every day.

If you believe that what you do makes a difference to how your life turns out then you're more likely to work for achievements, postpone gratification, set long-term goals, tolerate anxiety, benefit more from social support and spend more time studying and preparing for tests, thereby achieving more academically.

Research also shows that feeling in control buffers against stress and negative emotions, and increases energy and vigour. People who have higher levels of perceived control take greater responsibility for their health.

BOOST YOUR VITALITY

Vitality is associated with good physical health and wellbeing. It's an active positive state and so differs from happiness, which can include contentment and satisfaction (which are passive states). Virtually any factor that affects psychological and physical health also influences vitality – for example, depression, anxiety and stress. On top of this, health-related lifestyle choices, such as smoking, poor diet and lack of physical exercise can also result in lower vitality.

Vitality boosters

- Eat a balanced diet.
- Exercise regularly (see page 72).
- Get a good night's sleep (see page 60).
- Go for a walk in the fresh air.
- Participate in creative arts or music (see page 67).
- Laugh (see page 78).
- If you've been sitting down for a long time, get up and move around.

Vitality drainers to avoid

- Drinking alcohol.
- Eating a poor diet (particularly one low in iron).
- Irregular mealtimes.
- Poor sleep.
- Lack of physical exercise.
- Physical injury or chronic pain.
- Depression, anxiety and stress.

THINK HIGHLY OF YOURSELF

Think of the things that you are good at and try to see them as more important than the things you are not so good at.

Most people will dismiss their negative characteristics as inconsequential. Rather than being the sign of an egotistical or self-important person, this type of 'self-deception' is a healthy quality. In fact, there is evidence that people who are low in self-esteem or moderately depressed have more accurate self-perceptions!

Studies suggest that positive illusions are important for maintaining wellbeing, preserving self-esteem, and helping us to bond with each other. Positive illusions may also make us more creative and productive, as well as increasing our motivation and ability to persist at difficult tasks. All very good reasons to start thinking highly of yourself!

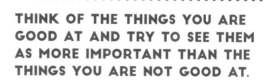

THINK OF THE THINGS YOU ARE GOOD AT AND TRY TO SEE THEM AS MORE IMPORTANT THAN THE THINGS YOU ARE NOT GOOD AT.

25

BE CURIOUS

Curiosity has driven explorers, scientists, artists and inventors to great achievements for centuries. We know that curiosity stimulates positive emotions and happiness. Inquisitive and interested people are more creative, feel less stress and boredom, and enjoy challenges. Curious children enjoy school more, have better relationships with their teachers and believe that they will achieve. Highly curious individuals also experience greater intimacy and attraction.

Supportive environments and finding an activity that is personally meaningful both influence how curious you are. So if you're a teacher or a boss, make sure your kids or employees feel safe and secure, since this is likely to foster curiosity and lead to an upward spiral of positive emotion.

I WONDER...

ACKNOWLEDGE THE NEGATIVE

Despite being unpleasant, negative emotions play an important role in our lives. Most people have heard of the 'fight-or-flight' response, attributed to American physiologist Walter Cannon at the beginning of the twentieth century. This connection between feeling and action has an evolutionary benefit: the negative emotion (such as 'I'm afraid') leads to an automatic response (the action of running away), which in a life or death situation would have enabled our ancestors to survive.

Negative emotions cause us to focus on a very narrow field of action and minimize distractions. This is why it's so incredibly difficult to be creative or innovative when you're feeling intensely pressured, and it's much easier to be grouchy and irritable. Studies show that people perform less well on simple tasks, like completing puzzles, when they feel negative. From a work perspective, if you want your team to perform at its best it's crucial to create the kind of environment that discourages negative emotions, or at least nips them in the bud.

Of course, few of us actively welcome negative emotions, although if we understand their presence from an evolutionary perspective and acknowledge that they are perfectly normal and acceptable, it can help. It's useful to remember that we can't dispel them all and we do need some negatives in order to fully appreciate the good things we have!

Negative emotion		Corresponding action
	Fear	Escape
	Anger	Attack
	Disgust	Expel

SEEK HELP IF YOU NEED IT

According to World Health Organisation experts, depression (by which we mean the debilitating mental condition that prevents us from carrying out normal daily activities for at least a few weeks) is the leading cause of disability worldwide. Only 30 per cent of the cases worldwide are properly diagnosed and treated, meaning that depression is probably the largest single cause of unhappiness in the world.

According to research, depression is associated with the presence of the 5-HTTLPR gene, which, when activated by highly stressful life events, can lead to full-blown depression. But if you have this gene, you needn't think you are destined to live an unhappy life. Depression can be avoided by steering clear of stressful situations, and, if this isn't possible, by actively seeking help from a medical practitioner or therapist. In this way, you can improve your chances of living a happy and fulfilling life, despite your situation and your genes.

BE HUMBLE

Humility is a characteristic we commonly associate with having a low opinion of oneself, being meek or lacking in self-esteem. But humility is a much more positive and interesting attribute than that. It's having an accurate (but not low) opinion of yourself and the ability to keep your talents and achievements in perspective. Being humble involves giving up the inclination to focus on yourself, and instead becoming more open to the importance, worth and potential of people around you.

How humility affects happiness

- Increased optimism.
- Improved friendships and intimate relationships.
- Greater satisfaction and morale at work.
- Openness to new experiences and new learning.
- Greater empathy, compassion and altruism.
- Decreased anxiety, fear and depression.
- Decreased conflict, anger and aggression.

ACCEPT THE UNCHANGEABLE

Acceptance is the experience of a (usually problematic) situation without trying to change it. It's not the same thing as 'giving up' or 'doing nothing'.

YOU MAY BE HAPPIER IF YOU LEARN HOW TO ACCEPT, RATHER THAN COPE WITH, A NEGATIVE SITUATION.

Often we talk about acceptance in terms of negative life experiences, such as bereavement, infidelity and ill health. In practical terms, it means being willing to experience typically uncomfortable thoughts and feelings without letting them dictate your behaviour.

You may be happier if you learn how to accept, rather than cope with, a negative situation. Studies on people with chronic pain syndrome showed that acceptance of chronic pain, as opposed to merely coping with the condition, was associated with less pain, disability, depression and anxiety and with better work status. So stop searching for an answer to problems and instead focus on other positive aspects of your everyday life.

DEVELOP YOUR RESILIENCE

Have you ever wondered how some people seem to bounce back from adversity, whereas others succumb to depression and go under? What is it about resilient people that enables them to pull through successfully, and in some cases, do even better than before?

Researchers believe that thinking style, optimism, temperament, self-control and sense of humour all contribute to their level of resilience, as do a positive family environment and supportive relationships. You can work on improving these, but you can also try to face problems head on, rather than simply giving up; you'll find it easier to bounce back after misfortune.

Happiness also enhances resilience, creating what's known as a virtuous circle. Resilient people experience more positive emotions and positive emotions protect us from depression and lead to increased optimism, wellbeing and tranquility.

RELIEVE STRESS

It's been long established that living or working in a stressful environment can have a negative impact on physical and psychological health. You can help ease stress in the short term using yoga, meditation, physical exercise and creative activities such as watercolour painting (see page 68). This won't eradicate it forever, though. In the longer term, you need to act on the source of the stress itself.

The first step is to identify what is causing the stress and then work out what you can do about it. Sometimes you can find a solution yourself, or you can talk to others about changing things. Whatever action you decide to take, remember that new activities and behaviours take time to settle in, so be prepared not to see the benefit immediately.

How to relieve stress
- Use relaxation techniques such as meditation (see page 93).
- Talk to someone supportive.
- Go for a walk or do physical exercise.
- Take up a relaxing hobby, such as watercolour painting.
- Accept practical help from friends or colleagues.
- Let off steam – for example, go where no one can hear you and scream, hit a cushion or use a stress ball.
- Know your limits – walk away from ultra-stressful situations until you have regained control.
- Take a vacation

CHOOSE WELL

It's a commonly held belief that more choice leads to greater freedom. Some choice is good for you; it gives you autonomy and enables you to exercise control over your life.

Research suggests that while some choice has a beneficial effect on our wellbeing, too much choice is bad for us. Being overloaded with choices results in a complete inability to choose, along with feelings of regret, raised expectations and blaming yourself when your decision turns out to be less than perfect. So, follow the advice below, give yourself fewer options and you'll find it easier to make decisions.

How to make good choices

- Learn to spend careful time over a choice only when it is worth it, for example, choosing a career.
- For unimportant decisions try to be satisfied with an option that is merely good enough, rather than trying to make absolutely the best choice.
- Lower your expectations – do not expect perfection, no matter how many choices there are.
- Once you've made up your mind, stick to it and stop looking at the alternatives!

USE YOUR TIME WISELY

For many of us in the Western world, work-life balance has become an organisational mantra in the last decade.

Even though we seem busier than ever, we actually have on average between five and seven hours more free time per week than we did in 1965. When people are asked to guess how much free time they have, typically they underestimate it by as much as 50 per cent. So how can we use our time fully?

Research shows that time management training has very little effect on our performance or on how effectively we use our time. What actually matters is our motivation, whether we have a choice about the things we do, and whether we have a proactive or reactive approach to time.

It's worth remembering that the most consistent difference between people who are happy with their time use and those who aren't is that the happy ones regularly take time out for themselves.

TAKE A DEEP BREATH

It's something of a mantra that controlling your breath will bring a sense of calm. Science proves it's an effective strategy for managing stress and anxiety, triggering neurons in the brain that tell the body it's time to relax.

For ultimate benefit, incorporate this breathing exercise into your everyday routine. It's up to you whether you practise this technique standing up, sitting in a chair, or lying on a mat on the floor. Whatever position you choose, make yourself as comfortable as possible, resting your arms and placing your feet roughly hip-width apart.

Steps for deep-breathing

1 Let your breath flow as deeply into your stomach as is comfortable, without forcing it.

2 Try breathing in through your nose and out through your mouth

3 Breathe in gently and regularly. You may want to count steadily from one to five.

4 Then, without pausing or holding your breath, let it flow out gently, counting from one to five again, if you find this helpful.

5 Keep doing this for three to five minutes.

SHOW YOUR GRATITUDE

As a child you may remember writing thank-you letters for birthday and Christmas presents. As an adult it's probably not something you do as frequently, if at all. It's not that you're not thankful for the things you have in life, just that you don't often stop to think about it.

Expressing gratitude, whether in writing or verbally, is one of the simplest but most effective ways to increase your happiness. There is overwhelming evidence that people with a grateful disposition are more enthusiastic, joyful, attentive, determined, interested, helpful, optimistic and energetic than those who aren't. Grateful people have been shown to be less depressed, anxious, lonely, envious and materialistic. So remember to practise an attitude of gratitude every day!

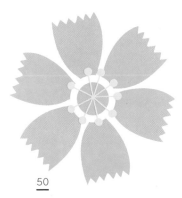

END EXPERIENCES ON A HIGH

One way we try to maximize our happiness is by lengenthening positive experiences, as it seems sensible that the length of time impacts how we remember it. A two-week vacation is surely twice as good as a one-week vacation in the same place, right?

Things aren't so straightforward. Our memory of an event is more affected by its peak and how it ends (the 'peak end' rule) than its duration. A one week vacation marred by atrocious weather that ended with a fantastic party would be remembered more favourably than one that was sunny throughout but ended in you having your wallet stolen.

Often we have to do things we don't want to do – visiting relatives in the hospital or giving a presentation at work. In these cases, try to see how you can ensure that the experience ends on a high, since this is what you will remember most.

OUR MEMORY OF AN EVENT IS MORE AFFECTED BY ITS PEAK AND HOW IT ENDS THAN ITS DURATION.

HAVE A GOOD CRY

The cathartic effects of releasing your emotions through tears have been documented in a study by Dr William Frey of Minnesota University, who found that emotional tears are chemically different from reflex tears (those stimulated by irritants such as smoke or chopping onions). Crying while angry, sad or distressed allows the eyes to secrete the stress hormones that have built up, explaining why you often feel better after crying even when the problem remains unchanged. Additional studies suggest that crying stimulates the production of endorphins, and crying is also a way of releasing pent-up emotion, re-establishing calm and relieving stress-related symptoms like heightened blood pressure and pulse rate.

So, don't bottle everything up. It's beneficial to have a good cry when you're feeling unhappy or stressed.

38

DAYDREAM

Daydreaming is one of life's great pleasures. Imagining an alternative reality and letting your thoughts meander fosters creativity and can focus our aspirations, improving life satisfaction.

In a series of questionnaire studies at York University, psychologist Raymond May found that people who daydreamed about their close family and friends reported higher levels of life satisfaction. While it can have a negative impact on happiness to fantasize about unobtainable relationships or ambitions, thinking freely and positively about potential scenarios in the near future enhances contentment.

Next time you're waiting for someone or on your way somewhere, think about all the positives in your life and welcome distractions into your thoughts: where might they take you next?

39

FORGIVE OTHERS
(AND YOURSELF)

We intuitively know that bearing grudges is harmful. But what if we understand forgiveness as something that you do for yourself and not for the person who has wronged you?

Studies show that the act of forgiving reduces anger, hostility, depression, anxiety and negative emotions, and that forgiving people are more likely to be agreeable, happier and more serene. Forgiveness is also linked to physical health such as reduced blood pressure levels, and it may aid in cardiovascular recovery from stress. Conversely, nursing grudges or dwelling on revenge only prevents you from moving on.

It is not just forgiving others that helps your wellbeing; forgiving yourself can also be very therapeutic.

How to enhance your forgiving side

- Write a letter of forgiveness (you don't have to send it).
- Forgive yourself for a past transgression.
- Read about public figures who have practised forgiveness such as Nelson Mandela or Mahatma Gandhi.
- Practise empathizing in your daily life – don't jump to conclusions if someone does something you don't understand.

LEARN HOW TO DEAL WITH PAINFUL EVENTS

At some point in our lives all of us will have to cope with misfortune and crises. Psychologists have identified three different ways we respond to a problem: we actively try to solve it; we deal with the emotions we feel; or we distract ourselves and pretend it doesn't exist.

If you're trying to solve a problem, it's important that you accept responsibility, develop a realistic plan and remain optimistic. If you procrastinate, remain pessimistic or don't follow plans through, the chances are that nothing changes, or the situation may deteriorate.

If you're dealing with the emotions, call on good friends for support or turn to relaxation or exercise. Research shows that relaxation enables us to cope better with stress, anxiety and pain while exercise reduces feelings of depression and releases endorphins in the brain. Catharsis can also be a beneficial form of emotional coping.

GROW YOUR MINDSET

Having a fixed mindset means that you have to keep succeeding in order to feel good about yourself, which is very difficult to maintain. Instead, Stanford University psychologist Carol Dweck identified the existence of a much more helpful frame of mind, called the 'growth mindset', in which people believe that their capabilities and potential can be enhanced and developed through practice and effort.

It's based on the fact that the human brain is an organ that continues to grow throughout our lives as we learn new things. For example, the auditory cortex of a musician's brain grows denser than that of a non-musician because of all the new neural connections made through musical practice. The more we learn the more connections are made in the brain, and the denser our brain grows. So it makes much more sense to adopt a 'growth mindset', one that allows you to try new ways of doing things if the first, second or third attempts fail.

The goals of people with a growth mindset are about learning and competence, not performance, so whether they succeed or fail, they'll still learn something new from the experience. Even better news is that learning goals have been shown to increase performance and enjoyment, and decrease negative emotion at the same time.

How to develop a growth mindset

- Remember that the brain, like any other human muscle, gets stronger the more you use it.
- Listen out for your 'fixed mindset voice' – the one that criticizes you for not succeeding, urges you to give up in the face of a setback or that says, 'if you were good enough you wouldn't have to try'.
- Recognize that it's up to you how you interpret challenges and setbacks.
- When times get tough, remember that people are successful because they persist. Even authors like John Grisham and J.K. Rowling were rejected by many publishers before finally getting a deal.
- Learn from setbacks – pick yourself up and try again.

WORRY LESS

Overthinking can make you feel pessimistic and self-critical, as well as undermining your motivation and concentration. But you can learn to overcome it as shown below.

How to escape the overthinking trap

1. Loosen the overthinking ties:
   a) Imagine a large red 'Stop' sign.
   b) Distract yourself.
   c) Set aside 30 minutes a day specifically for worrying, and only worry then.
   d) Talk to a trusted friend who can help you dispute your thoughts.
   e) Write your negative thoughts down.
2. Take action – every small step you take to solve the problem will be a step towards greater wellbeing.
3. Avoid overthinking traps – write a list of the specific triggers for your over-thinking (for example, specific times of the day or places) and avoid them in future.
4. Ask yourself whether what you are worrying about will really matter in a year's time. If the answer is 'yes', then focus your thinking on what you can learn from the experience.

FOCUS ON THE PRESENT

Scientists have discovered that how we perceive time can have a huge impact on our levels of happiness.

Studies show that 'past' people can focus in either a positive and sentimental way, or in a negative way. The former group have good relationships with family and friends, and fond memories; but the latter focus on unpleasant experiences and feel bitter as a result. 'Present' people might 'seize the day' but are at greater risk from temptations such as alcohol and drugs. 'Future' people delay current gratification and focus on goals and rewards. They tend to be more successful, but are at risk of becoming workaholics.

So which of the three is the most likely to lead to happiness? Experts suggest that a balanced time perspective – adapting your outlook to your current situation – offers the most advantages. So when you're playing with the kids or on vacation, focus on the present, enjoy the moment and don't let other issues encroach. At work, focus on being as productive as possible and put other problems out of your mind. And when thinking about your past, acceptance (see page 44)and forgiveness (see page 54) are crucial to your happiness.

FOCUS ON THE PRESENT, ENJOY THE MOMENT AND DON'T LET OTHER ISSUES ENCROACH

44

GET A GOOD NIGHT'S SLEEP

As those who struggle to get a good night's sleep know, the more you try to fall asleep the worse it tends to get. Sleep disorders are usually a symptom of an underlying issue, such as depression or stress, so even taking sleeping pills is often ineffective in the longer term.

Try to aim for six to eight and a half hours per night, as people who sleep for this length of time on average report the best levels of psychological and subjective wellbeing. They also report fewer symptoms of depression and anxiety, more positive relations with others, plus greater levels of control and purpose in their lives.

How to improve your sleep
- Establish a winding-down routine.
- When lying in bed, don't focus on what went wrong during the day.
- Avoid caffeinated drinks.
- Don't eat too close to bedtime.
- Exercise regularly.
- Don't clock-watch.
- Go to bed and get up at the same time every day, including weekends.

45

BUILD A ROUTINE

A routine is a series of habits that you practise everyday. While a routine of unhealthy habits has the potential to disrupt your happiness, a good routine which establishes structure provides comfort and can be both freeing and uplifting.

This is firstly because not having to think about the small decisions of everyday life releases your brain to think creatively or consider more meaningful things. You might also want to build into your routine time for rest or relaxation, or incorporate a hobby you want to try: practise makes perfect, as the saying goes, and doing something routinely will ensure you improve at it, with benefits for self-esteem and stress levels.

DANCE MORE

Dancing is fantastic for keeping you physically healthy: US research shows that a vigorous dance class can burn as many calories as a gym workout, while a study of older people found that dancing significantly reduced levels of unhealthy fats in the blood.

Learning new routines also keeps your brain sharp and in addition to the physical benefits, there is growing evidence that dancing is good for your psychological health. Dance and movement therapy is based on the premise that expressing yourself through bodily movement may have a secondary effect on your mental and emotional wellbeing.

Studies show that hip-hop dancing has a more positive impact on wellbeing than either ice-skating or body conditioning, and that afterwards psychological distress and fatigue are lower. You may experience improved self-esteem and com- munication from taking part in aerobic dancing, as well as heightened feelings of wellbeing and a sense of accomplishment. Whatever dance you're into, you can be sure that it contributes enormously to both your mental and physical fitness.

GET OUT IN THE GARDEN

Gardening is an opportunity for personal growth, self-expression and finding meaning. There's nothing quite like getting outside and getting your hands dirty, absorbing the abundance of colours, textures and scents and appreciating being so close to nature.

Regular gardening helps keep you physically healthy, specifically reducing heart disease and cholesterol levels, improving diabetes care, manual dexterity and coordination skills.

Possibly because plants require active nurturing, studies show that gardening greatly benefits your mental health, decreasing stress and depression and increasing self-esteem, resulting in a significant improvement in positive emotion and psychological wellbeing. So, whether you've got a window box, a handful of containers, a small yard or an acre of prime soil at your fingertips, get your rubber clogs on, go out there and get gardening!

LIVE HAPPY

TRY A NEW HOBBY

Many people complain about the long hours they work and consequently how little time they have to do the things they love, whether it's playing with the kids, taking salsa lessons, collecting memorabilia or researching family history. Whatever your hobby, remember the quote, 'nobody ever said on their deathbed, "I wish I'd spent more time in the office"'.

We believe that we work longer hours than ever before, but statistics show that for most of us over the past 30 or 40 years our leisure time has actually increased.

Studies of time use and time perspectives reveal that the amount of time needed to spend on leisure activities in order to feel satisfied varies greatly from person to person. The trick is to find the right balance. You don't want to pursue your hobby so enthusiastically that it starts eating into working hours, neither do you want it leaving you with little time for your partner and kids.

What is it about a hobby that is good for us? The key is whether or not the activity triggers our interest. Interest is accompanied by positive emotions like enjoyment and surprise, which often cause us to explore further, adopt new behaviours or pick up new knowledge. This in turn increases our curiosity, which can be beneficial to our happiness (see page 39). Experiencing these positive emotions builds enduring personal resources in a virtuous cycle, creating a true win/win situation, so get out there and find your perfect hobby.

Suggested hobbies to improve your happiness
- Watercolour painting (it's all in the body movement).
- Sculpting or making pottery.
- Gardening (see page 63).
- Scrapbooking (it's all about keeping happy memories).
- Singing in a choir.
- Joining a dance class (see page 62).
- Knitting.
- Learning a musical instrument.
- Doing some yoga.
- Doing puzzles.

VISIT AN ART GALLERY

SMILE

Research suggests that visiting an art gallery, even for a brief trip of about 40 minutes, can significantly reduce the level of the stress hormone cortisol in your body.

In a London study, participants reported a 45 per cent reduction in their perceived stress levels. What is also interesting is that the drop in cortisol levels was not only very substantial (about 32 per cent) but also very quick. Immediately following the gallery visit, stress hormone levels had fallen to below average for the time of day, whereas under normal circumstances it would take about five hours for them to fall to this level.

So, next time you're having a demanding day, think about popping along to your local art gallery for a cup of decaf and a de-stress at lunchtime, or even on the way home. Whether you want to gaze at the Gainsboroughs, peruse the Pollocks or marvel at the Monets, it'll do you good.

MAKE MUSIC

Music is a powerful mood modifier, capable of generating intense emotions. Many of us have some kind of relationship with music even if we're not accomplished performers. We may sing in the bath, tap our fingers to a beat, hum along to the radio or stream music on our phones as we commence the long commute.

Music features largely at important life events: singing Happy Birthday for example, or playing the wedding march at a marriage ceremony. Music is also intensely individual; there seems to be something out there for every taste. It has such a significant cultural impact that young people in the West in particular use music as a means of finding their identity.

We know intuitively that music plays a tremendously important role in how we feel and behave from day to day, and science confirms this. Studies have shown that participating in music, for example singing in a choir, can lead to significant feelings of joy, elation and excitement, positive feelings about life, and losing your sense of self. In addition, participating in a musical performance can lead to greater physical wellbeing, sociability and positive outlook.

LIVE HAPPY

51

BE MORE CREATIVE

Feeling positive and upbeat increases creativity, whereas negative emotions often stifle it. In studies, groups of participants watched five-minute video clips that induced either a positive or a neutral mood. Those who watched the comedy clip performed better on tasks that required them to solve a problem creatively than those who watched the neutral clip. If you don't have access to funny or happy footage, you could think of a happy memory or a person you love.

It's not just happiness that makes you more creative: doing creative activities can help improve your mood, and even help you cope with a traumatic experience.

CREATIVE ACTIVITIES SUCH AS SINGING OR LISTENING TO MUSIC CAN BE A POWERFUL MOOD MODIFIER. PLUS IF YOU'RE BEING CREATIVE WITH OTHERS, YOU GET THE BENEFIT OF SPENDING TIME WITH FRIENDS.

While the majority of studies into the impact of creative activities on both physical and psychological wellbeing have been conducted with participants who are suffering from a mental illness of some kind, it may be that the therapeutic effects of creativity (such as absorption, engagement, greater self-esteem and enhancement of perceived control, as well as increased energy and happiness) could be equally well experienced by people who are mentally healthy. This is something that researchers need to look at in more depth, but it has been established that doing other creative activities such as singing or listening to music can be a powerful mood modifier, plus if you're being creative with others, such as in a class or just with friends, you get the benefit of spending time with others (see page 94). So, get drawing on your own or with a friend, write down your thoughts in a letter or a diary (see page 76) and find other ways to be more creative.

BE PLAYFUL

Play is essential to the successful development of any species. It provides the young with a relatively risk-free opportunity to learn about the world and experiment with new behaviours. It's a way to develop social competence before it really begins to matter.

Play is not only both non-serious and functional, but it is also adaptive, as some scientists suggest: for example, play-fighting is a way to practise real-life hunting skills, which would have ensured the survival of the species thousands of years ago.

Playing brings a great many benefits both in the short and long term. It's fun, it's risk-free, it allows you to be creative and break out of your normal boundaries, it reduces stress, and it gives you the opportunity to develop new skills. Whether you're six or 106, playing is most definitely good for you, so go and have some fun.

ENJOY A GLASS OF WINE

Many of us enjoy an alcoholic drink every now and then and moderate drinking is widely thought to be beneficial to health and happiness. Studies consistently show that drinking one unit a day, especially of red wine, is linked to better physical health.

There is a known association between alcohol and depression that is often described as 'J shaped', meaning that people who drink moderate amounts of alcohol have lower rates of depression and anxiety disorders than those who are teetotalers, while those who drink excessive amounts have the highest depression rates of all. So the best advice for your physical health and happiness is to enjoy a drink in moderation!

How to drink safely

- Use soft drink or water spacers to pace yourself.
- Drink plenty of water, especially before you go to bed.
- Eat before you drink; food will soak up the alcohol.
- Don't mix your drinks.
- Stick to the recommended limits – try not to exceed more than one or two alcoholic beverages daily.
- Don't drink and drive.

EXERCISE REGULARLY

While the definition of what counts as physical exercise (i.e., moderate or strenuous activity) varies depending on which expert you ask, all health professionals agree that doing some form of exercise on a regular basis is essential to keep the mind and the body fit and healthy.

There is mounting evidence to suggest exercise can mitigate against psychological as well as physical illness. In one study, participants diagnosed with depression were randomly assigned to medication, exercise, or a combination of both. Ten months later recurrence rates for the medication-only group were 38 per cent, for the combination group 31 per cent and for the exercise-only group 9 per cent. The message here is that physical exercise is an absolute must not only for your physical health but also your mental wellbeing.

HAPPINESS

SMILE MORE

How often do you smile every day? Research proves what Darwin suggested as far back as the 1870s, that showing your emotions physically intensifies them – so smiling can actually increase your wellbeing.

In quirky experiments involving holding a pencil in the mouth to simulate either a smile or a frown, scientists have shown that if you physically mimic a smile, your brain can be tricked into believing that you're actually feeling this emotion.

But it's no good smiling half-heartedly. Your smile needs to be genuine, with you lips drawn back, cheeks raised and wrinkles appearing around the eyes.

In case you find it a bit tricky to generate a genuine grin without prompting, why not keep a few funny photos in your wallet or on your desk to get you started, or get a book of jokes to keep in the office for whenever you feel in need of an instant pick-me-up.

56

PUT DOWN YOUR DEVICES

Technology has its advantages. It can be used as a means to share knowledge, stay in touch with people around the globe and make new connections. Still, prolonged use and attention to smartphones and other devices can have negative results on subjective wellbeing and lead to feelings of low mood.

This is partly due to the mental state of permanent activity that constant connectivity induces: continually checking for social media and news updates not only means we are more distracted, but also decreases our engagement in the everyday world around us, affecting our relationships.

Research has also revealed a negative impact on our memory, our ability to process information and general intelligence when our smartphone is even just in our sights, rather than in a bag or another room.

So, make sure to have some downtime from your devices and hide them away for at least part of the day, especially before bed (see page 60).

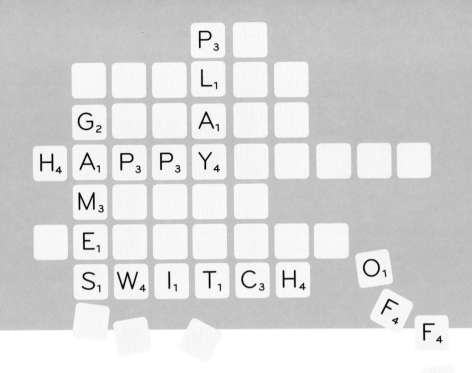

How to moderate your habits

- Don't check your phone the minute you wake up, or in the hour before you go to sleep.
- Sleep in a different room to your devices to minimize the chance of them interrupting your sleep.
- Consider downloading an app that tracks how much time you spend on your device so you can monitor and reduce your usage.
- Delete any time-wasting or particularly distracting apps. If you can't quite face this, at least turn off notifications so that you are more in control of when you check for updates.

KEEP A DIARY

The process of writing has long been believed to be a cathartic experience. If you write about an unpleasant or traumatic experience in a structured way (organizing and integrating what happened) then evidence suggests this activity can be beneficial in the long term. Not only can it help you find the necessary insight to overcome the painful emotions or thoughts associated with the experience, it can also improve your physical health and enable you to regain a sense of wellbeing.

Be careful to write about experiences that are upsetting in a more free-form way, because it's possible to get stuck in a cycle dwelling on what went wrong, without acquiring the perception needed to move on.

In terms of happy life events, rather than just writing it all down, it's more important that you also replay what happened in your mind, reliving and savouring the moment without trying to determine its causes or meanings. By taking time to really appreciate the occasion in this way, you'll maintain or even increase your positive emotions associated with the happy memory.

BE MINDFUL

Mindfulness is more than merely relishing or basking in the moment; it's about really noticing, appreciating and enhancing the positive experiences in your life. In being mindful you slow down intentionally, consciously pay attention to all your senses (touch, taste, sight, sound and smell). You stretch out the experience and concentrate on noticing what it is about the experience that you enjoy. It works for anything, whether it's as simple as stroking the cat or musing over the time you scored a hat-trick for the school hockey team.

Put some of your hard-earned leisure time to good use, to start savouring the moment rather than rushing to complete the next task. Mindfulness helps you appreciate your everyday life more, it makes time appear to slow down, and boosts your happiness into the bargain. What could be better than that?

LAUGH MORE

Laughter is beneficial to physical and mental fitness, so we should aim to laugh more each day. Studies have shown that even faking laughter can work, by tricking your brain into thinking it's real. And it's not just your mood that can be improved – see below.

How laughter improves your happiness

- Acts as a coping mechanism which reduces depression and stress.
- Relieves hay fever symptoms, decreases pain and allows us to tolerate discomfort more easily.
- Helps protect against illness.
- Aids healing after operations and illnesses by stimulating our immune system.
- Reduces blood sugar levels.
- Increases positive emotions, which in turn can boost our creativity.
- Sharpens up our problem-solving skills.
- Releases tension.
- Brings people together.

TURN OFF THE TV

People who watch less than half an hour of TV a day are more satisfied with their lives than people who watch more than this.

Research suggests that TV rarely portrays reality and there is much more violence, unstable relationships, affluent people and luxury than there is in real life, which can give us a warped perception. For example, people who watch a lot of television tend to overestimate crime rates and other people's wealth, place more importance on material goods and are less satisfied with their own income.

On top of this, TV viewing is a passive activity for most of us, and doesn't require any skill. We can easily become apathetic and bored, which all contributes to lower subjective wellbeing. So chances are that doing something else with your time, like going for a run or calling a friend, will be more beneficial to your wellbeing. Avoid watching TV every night and be mindful of the choices you're making. Select the programmes you want to watch at the start of the week and stick to them and try not to channel-surf.

BE MORE OPTIMISTIC

Are you a 'glass half full' person? The type who looks on the bright side of life, rather than worrying over all the what-might-have-beens or what-ifs?

If so, optimism is very good news for both your mental and physical wellbeing. Research has shown that when dealing with difficulties in their lives, optimistic people experience less distress, anxiety and depression than do pessimistic people. But optimists don't necessarily see the world through rose-tinted glasses. They heed health warnings and take action towards greater physical wellbeing, just as pessimists do.

A small proportion of people use defensive pessimism as a beneficial coping strategy. This involves setting unrealistically low expectations to help prepare for the worst, even when previous performance has been good. Rather than sending them into a spiral of negativity, this pessimistic behaviour allows them to avoid getting caught up in their emotions and in fact enables them to act more effectively.

Nevertheless, being an optimist has many of its own benefits, so if you would like to learn how to reverse pessimism and be more optimistic, read on. Optimists learn from negative events, persist longer at difficult tasks and tend not to give up, believing the situation can be handled one way or another.

OPTIMISTS LEARN FROM NEGATIVE EVENTS, PERSIST LONGER AT DIFFICULT TASKS AND TEND NOT TO GIVE UP.

How to become more optimistic

- Build awareness of your Automatic Negative Thoughts (ANTs). Wear an elastic band on your wrist and snap it every time you think something negative.

- When things go wrong, dispute any pessimistic explanations you have – what other possible explanations could there be? What would it be more useful to believe? Disputation becomes easier with practice.

- Deliberately put aside worrisome thoughts until later – this leaves you free to act in the present.

62

CHERISH YOUR RELATIONSHIPS

Human beings are social animals – the future of the human race is dependent on us finding mates we can love and live with, so we can reproduce and bring up our children in a loving and protected environment so that they too can be happy and successful in love. But love is a double-edged sword, as you will also know if you've ever experienced unrequited love or been dumped or divorced by a partner. At these times, love brings anything but happiness.

According to researchers Baumeister and Leary, humans have a fundamental need to belong. So it's not surprising that in studies, people in a relationship are happier than those who are not. We don't yet know whether people who are satisfied with their romantic partner are happier, or whether people who are happier are more satisfied with their relationships. Regardless, love and happiness are a match, so spend time with your loved ones and work on building loving relationships with your friends, family or partner.

ENJOY SEX

For many people, having a satisfying sex life seems to be a fundamental part of what it means to be happy, but there is evidence that for some people, sex isn't actually such a big deal. Providing they're matched with a partner who feels the same, infrequent sex will not cause any problem for their relationship or their emotional wellbeing. And many people make celibacy a life choice, and manage perfectly happily without sex at all.

How can sex make you happy?

Studies suggest that sex is an important part of creating and maintaining positive human relationships because it fulfils three basic psychological needs:

- **Intimacy:** being loved, desired and respected satisfies the need to feel close to other people.
- **Control:** when both partners can talk to each other openly about their sexual desires and agree on what they do in bed, their need to feel that their activities are self-chosen and self-endorsed is fulfilled.
- **Competency:** for all its apparent mystery, sex is a skill like any other; the more you practise the better you get, thus fulfilling the need to feel competent.

LIVE WITH OTHERS

Although the number of adults who choose to live together rather than marry varies widely from country to country, cohabiting has increased dramatically in industrialized countries over the past 50 years. For many couples, cohabitation is an alternative to marriage, for others it's usually a precursor to marriage. The increasing number of people who live together suggests that it makes them happy – why else would they do it?

We already know that spending time with others can improve your wellbeing (see page 94) and living with a partner can also affect your happiness. The happiness of cohabiting couples does seem to depend on what kind of culture they live in.

Overall, cohabiting people are happier on the whole than the single, divorced or widowed. Generally, however, they are not as happy as married couples, and they're more likely to suffer from depression than either the married, the never married or people who have divorced once.

SMALL ACTS OF KINDNESS

Doing good deeds often not only boosts your mood temporarily, it also leads to long-lasting happiness, as well as making other people feel good. Scientific studies also show that acts of kindness have more impact on your wellbeing if you do a variety of different things, rather than repeating the same activity a number of times. It's a brilliant win-win activity, plus it doesn't have to cost you anything.

Why kind acts make you happier

Researchers suggest a number of reasons why doing kind acts for others makes you happier:

- It may make you feel more confident, in control and optimistic about your ability to make a difference.
- It enables you to connect with other people (a basic human need).
- It may make you feel more positive about other people and the community you live in, and foster cooperation between people.

GET HITCHED!

25%

PERCENTAGE OF
NEVER MARRIED WOMEN
'VERY HAPPY'

43%

PERCENTAGE OF
MARRIED WOMEN
'VERY HAPPY'

38%

PERCENTAGE OF
MARRIED MEN
'VERY HAPPY'

20%

PERCENTAGE OF
NEVER MARRIED MEN
'VERY HAPPY'

It's been long established in the psychology world that having close and loving relationships and feeling more secure and attached to other people are fundamental human needs. Human beings need other people to survive, not just for procreation but also for the psychological support that you get from livings with others.

We know that types of marriage and long-term partnership vary across the globe, but one of the most reliable findings is that people who are married are happier than those who aren't. For the romantics among you, this may well confirm what you always believed, that traditional relationships are the best ones. At the same time, this evidence doesn't prove definitively that getting married will make you happier; it may be that being married makes you happier, or it may be that happier people are more likely to get married in the first place.

KEEP MOVING FORWARDS

It's not a simple case of 'relationship equals happiness', even if this is what often gets portrayed in romantic fiction. While getting married can make you happier, being in an unhappy relationship is worse for you than being single or divorced.

What's more, the state of your relationship affects how satisfied you are with life in general: only 3 per cent of those in a 'not too happy' marriage, for example, were very satisfied with their lives as a whole, compared to 10 per cent of people in 'pretty happy' marriages and 57 per cent in 'very happy' marriages.

HAPPY COUPLES CREATE A 'BANK ACCOUNT' OF POSITIVE FEELINGS ABOUT THEIR PARTNER.

So what contributes to a satisfying and long-lasting relationship? Physical attractiveness, sexual compatibility and similar attitudes, interests and values are all important. Happy couples also create a 'bank account' of positive feelings about their partner, which they can draw on, especially during times of conflict.

68

AFFIRM YOUR BELIEF

Religious and spiritual people tend to be happier than those who aren't. As well as a more well-defined system of beliefs and values, higher levels of hope and optimism and better coping styles, it's been suggested that the social and emotional support provided by faith communities also contributes to greater wellbeing. In studies, the frequency with which members of faith communities attend their church, temple or other religious setting also has been found to be significantly connected to happiness.

Religious groups are often fairly homogenous, so members may feel that their beliefs, values and life choices are constantly being affirmed, leading to improved self-esteem and confidence. But it's not just the people who receive social and emotional support from their religious community who benefit; research also indicates that volunteering and helping others in a spiritual setting benefits the providers of the support as much as it does the recipients.

RESOLVE FAMILY FIGHTS

Arguing with family is almost inevitable. It's a normal part of growing up and finding your independence. Research shows that adolescents argue more with their mothers than they do with their fathers or siblings. It shouldn't be surprising to find that family differences turn out to have an impact on teenagers' wellbeing; resolving conflicts with parents is linked to greater wellbeing when measured in terms of self-esteem, depression and risky behaviour (taking drugs, drinking, etc.). In particular, because the subject of arguments with mothers tend to be of a personal nature, such as choice of friends and appearance, it's easy to see why these types of conflict would have an impact on self-esteem and why resolving them has a greater benefit.

THE QUALITY OF OUR LIVES DEPENDS NOT ON WHETHER WE HAVE CONFLICTS, BUT ON HOW WE RESPOND TO THEM. TOM CRUM

We don't yet know whether it's failing to resolve conflicts that causes lower wellbeing, or whether adolescents with lower wellbeing are less likely to resolve the conflicts. Either way, we should all work to ensure that any family fights are settled constructively.

COMMUNICATE AT WORK

COMMUNICATION WORKS FOR THOSE WHO WORK AT IT

JOHN POWELL

Everyone experiences conflict in the workplace. It can crop up between individuals for all sorts of reasons, such as having different ideas on how to complete a task, or differences over personal beliefs and values. Research indicates that the latter types of problem, those based on interpersonal relationships, cause conflict stress, by triggering feelings of reduced control and undermining your sense of self, resulting in tension, anxiety, stress and reduced wellbeing.

Not all employees are adversely affected by relationship conflict at work, since individual personality characteristics lead to different interpretations and reactions. Since we often don't know how people will react to stress until it's too late, many employers are proactively training their managers in mediation skills, which can prevent the occurrence of conflicts in the first place. If your workplace doesn't offer training programmes, you can still learn mediation skills from courses, books and online sources to help you in the workplace.

71

TAKE CARE OF AN ANIMAL

Spending time with animals confers a number of physical health benefits, such as reducing blood pressure, heart rate, stress and depression. But there may also be mental benefits; studies indicate that assistance dogs such as guide dogs for the blind have a positive influence on the self-esteem and wellbeing of people with disabilities. Owning and caring for a dog has more beneficial effects on our physical and mental health than owning a cat, although the reasons for this are not yet entirely clear. Dr Deborah Wells of Queen's University, Belfast, suggests that dogs can aid our health by preventing minor ailments such as colds and headaches, facilitating recovery from illness, and helping to predict certain ailments, such as epileptic seizures.

It's likely that promenading in the local park brings you into contact with other dog owners, thus fulfiling the fundamental human need of connecting with other people. Research may not yet give us all the answers, but owning and caring for a much-loved pet can do wonders for your physical health and may do the same for your happiness.

72

DEVELOP EMOTIONALLY

Emotional intelligence is the capacity to recognize and manage our and others' emotions. If we can identify emotional messages in the expression and tone of others, we're more likely to understand their perspective and empathize. Managing our emotions effectively – improving a bad mood, relaxing when nervous or remaining calm when angry, is the crux of emotional intelligence and can increase our chances of happiness.

How to manage your emotions

- Give yourself a pep-talk – or find a friend to give you one.
- Change position – get up from your desk, look up, stretch and walk around.
- Go outside if you can, or get some physical exercise.
- Don't resort to drink, drugs or comfort food.
- Listen to some relaxing music.
- Don't avoid the person or thing that has upset you.
- Meditate (see page 93).
- Find a pleasant distraction – spend an hour on your favourite hobby or run an errand for someone.
- Find a friend to chat with.

73

START YOUR DAY WITH MEDITATION

Meditation, the practice of focusing your attention, has been around for many thousands of years and is typically associated with Buddhism. It is becoming increasingly popular in the Western world, particularly the technique of mindfulness: the focus of thoughts in the present moment. Scientific studies on meditation report enhanced resilience, reduced stress, greater awareness of subtle emotions, greater energy and enthusiasm for life and an increased ability to relax.

How to practise zazen (sitting) meditation

Practise for 3 to 5 minutes at first, building up to 20 minutes a day when you feel ready.

- Adopt a comfortable kneeling position. Keep your spine erect and your shoulders aligned.
- Look ahead with your eyes half-closed. Soften your gaze. It helps to be facing a blank wall so as to avoid visual distractions.
- Take your focus inside and notice your breath moving in and out. Calmly move into witnessing mode: watching your thoughts, emotions and sensations as if you were a distinterested observer. When a train of thought carries you away, simply acknowledge it, ask it to pass through, and return to the awareness of your breath.
- When it's time to finish, come back to an awareness of the room and your body. Sit in quiet reflection for a while before re-entering the world.

SPEND TIME WITH FRIENDS

The quality of our relationships with others can have a significant impact on our general wellbeing, and having close friends in whom we can confide is a very important source of happiness. In one study carried out on 222 college students it was found that the key difference between the happiest 10 per cent of the group and the rest of them was that the former had rich and satisfying interpersonal lives. They also spent the least time alone and the most time socialising, and were rated highest on good relationships by themselves and by others.

HAVING A SMALL NUMBER OF INTIMATE FRIENDS YOU CAN CONFIDE IN IS MORE BENEFICIAL TO YOUR HAPPINESS THAN HAVING A LARGER GROUP OF CASUAL ACQUAINTANCES.

The number of close friends people have typically seems to be pretty small. This is completely normal and in fact having a smaller number of intimate friends who you can trust and confide in is more beneficial to your happiness than having a larger group of more casual acquaintances.

Studies have shown that adolescents spend approximately 30 per cent of their time with friends, whereas adults spend less than 10 per cent. This is likely because we spend more time on adult responsibilities, such as work and spending time with family, partners and children.

Best friends are those who bring out the best in us, who we can depend on come what may, and who are kind, loving, honest and loyal to us. Research shows that these qualities are far more important in explaining a best friendship than features like the friend's accomplishments, attractiveness or status. So, despite the pressures of life and our apparent busyness (see page 113), be sure to make time for the friendships in your life.

How friendships can make you happy

- They fulfil the human need to feel that you belong somewhere.
- Friendships provide social support.
- Happy people make more desirable friends than unhappy people, so therefore they're more often selected as companions by others.

AVOID COMPARISON

We wouldn't be human if we didn't occasionally compare ourselves with other people, but it can become a problem when we do it too frequently or against people whose situations aren't relevant to our own.

While it's fine to make the occasional comparison with friends, neighbours or colleagues, it is all too easy now to compare ourselves to people who are clearly not in our reference group, given the prevalence of advertising and social media. Upward comparison with people who earn three, five or 10 times our salaries or more can only lead to greater dissatisfaction and lower levels of happiness as we judge ourselves against them.

Let's face it, there will always be someone who is more beautiful, more intelligent, slimmer, richer or healthier than us, but that doesn't mean we're lacking!

KEEP THINGS IN PERSPECTIVE

Happy and unhappy people tend to approach comparison in different ways. It's not that happy people don't make comparisons; they do. However, other people's successes and failures don't diminish or augment their own. Unhappy people on the other hand feel bad when they see that someone else is more successful (in whatever avenue) than they are; it can make them feel inferior, envious or resentful, as well as lowering their self-esteem. So, try to focus on your own successes and maintain a level of balance about the situation. It may be that you're not seeing the bigger picture or that you are judging the outcome by the wrong yardstick.

Ways to see the bigger picture

- Consider taking a break, going on a retreat or travelling somewhere new to refresh your perspective.
- Think about your trajectory and imagine what your life would look like in 10 years' time if you stayed on the same path. Don't catastrophize. Instead, notice your emotions and take the appropriate steps.
- Acknowledge that there will always be someone better off in some way than you.
- Notice when you start to make upward comparisons and distract yourself with another activity.
- Avoid situations that lead to comparison. For instance, stop buying celebrity magazines or newspaper 'rich lists'.

BE HAPPY FOR OTHERS

When you share good news with others or celebrate the event, you experience additional happiness, possibly because in retelling the event, you re-experience it. The more people you tell, the more your happiness increases. Researchers have also suggested that sharing or celebrating good news with other people strengthens social relationships and builds trust and self-esteem.

IF YOU WANT OTHERS TO BE HAPPY, PRACTISE COMPASSION. IF YOU WANT TO BE HAPPY, PRACTISE COMPASSION.

DALAI LAMA

The response you get from the people you share the news with is crucial. If they react enthusiastically, openly showing that they're pleased for you by talking positively about your success, your wellbeing will be enhanced. On the other hand, if they react negatively, either by actively scoffing at your success, or by ignoring it, your sense of wellbeing is likely to be reduced.

So next time you have good news, make sure you share it with as many of your friends as possible. And when someone shares their good news with you, be genuinely pleased for them; you'll be making them happier in the process.

SET ACHIEVABLE GOALS

Some psychologists suggest that the ability to reflect, choose a direction in life and be motivated to pursue certain goals is key for psychological wellbeing. The crucial thing is not what the goal is or even whether it's actually achieved, but whether the action of pursuing it helps you meet basic psychological needs.

Engaging in activities that are intrinsically motivating leads to greater satisfaction and better physical and psychological wellbeing. Studies of weight loss or alcohol treatment programmes show that people who are motivated to pursue goals are more likely to succeed, and less likely to relapse.

How having a goal increases happiness

- Autonomy: being free to choose what you want to do.
- Competence: feeling effective.
- Pleasure-stimulation: sense of having fun.
- Physical health.
- Security: having a sense of order in life.
- Self-esteem: feeling worthy.
- Self-actualization: a sense that you are growing towards an ideal self or world.
- Relatedness: feeling connected to others

LEARN SOMETHING NEW

Although empirical research has discovered that IQ and happiness aren't linked, there is a small correlation between education and happiness.

In poorer countries, education confers disproportionate benefits. If you live in an underdeveloped country you stand a much better chance of satisfying the basic physical needs of finding food and shelter if you're educated. The benefits of education are also related to occupational status and income; if you're very poor, earning more money does bring greater happiness. It's just that this is only true up to a point, after which the increases in happiness start to level out (see page 24).

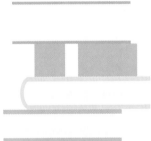

Education can also be a means to greater individual freedom and empowerment. Making progress towards desired goals has also been shown to lead to great levels of psychological wellbeing. You can attend courses, enrole in online programmes or download apps to learn new skills, such as a new language, playing a musical instrument, or taking a cooking class. There is no limit to what you can learn.

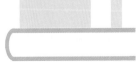

GET THINGS DONE

Psychologists have found that it is not so much the completion of a goal that matters, but the progress you make towards it (see page 99). The key to making progress with 'big' goals is to break them down into small manageable steps.

How to get things done

- If you are stuck on a particular goal and seem unable to make any headway, try to break it down into smaller steps.
- Review your progress frequently – constantly ask yourself what you could do differently.
- Don't be afraid to ask for help.
- If you can, delegate the task (or parts of it). Ask someone to help you and do the job together.
- Make chores fun by finding new ways to do them. For example, make it into a competition – time yourself doing the weeding or cleaning and see if you can do it quicker next time.

STEP UP AT WORK

Job satisfaction and wellbeing have less to do with salary or status of a job, and more to do with how much control you have over the type of work you do every day and how meaningful your job is (see page 36). Even though the amount of stress you experience day-to-day tends to increase as you rise through the ranks, so too does your autonomy, and it is this, or the lack of it, that affects your wellbeing and satisfaction at work.

Expectation of job loss, however, appears to have one of the largest negative effects on job satisfaction, and thus on wellbeing, although there are other factors, including increasing stress, responsibility and effort. Feeling secure at work, on the other hand, leads to increased psychological wellbeing and greater job satisfaction. Just as happiness is 'U-shaped' in age, so is the perception of job security; it starts high in young adulthood, reaching a low point in one's 40s, then increases steadily up to retirement.

In studies of job satisfaction and happiness it was found that the majority of workers are actually pretty satisfied at work. The European Social Survey has compared people's job satisfaction and found a slight increase in their average scores over time (where 0 is 'extremely dissatisfied' and 10 is 'extremely satisfied').

It's clear that there is a link between job satisfaction and sense of autonomy. So if you're looking to improve overall wellbeing, consider how your situation at work is impacting your happiness. Initiative and a sense of achievement appear to be the most important aspects of wellbeing at work; you're likely to get these through more responsibility. Volunteer yourself for a new project, or start working towards a promotion. You'll get a sense of achievement from your successes at work when you've overcome these challenges.

		2006		2010	
		Men	**Women**	**Men**	**Women**
Satisfied with Work	Full-time	6.8	6.8	7.3	7.2
	Part-time	7.0	7.4	7.1	7.3
Satisfied with Work-life Balance	Full-time	5.8	5.3	6.2	5.8
	Part-time	7.3	6.9	6.9	7.0

LEARN TO LIKE YOURSELF

Self-esteem is generally high in childhood, then takes a battering during adolescence, gradually increasing again in early- to mid-adulthood, before starting to decline as we enter old age.

Studies have found a significant relationship between self-esteem and happiness. An analysis of 137 different personality traits found that self-esteem again was one of the strongest predictors. But while this evidence shows how important self-esteem is for happiness, some psychologists are very against it: some people can have overzealous high self-esteem, which can be unstable and sometimes leads people to conclude that they are doing better than they are, giving them an exaggerated sense of self-importance. So, learning to like yourself can be beneficial to your health, but make sure that you don't lose sight of the bigger picture: focus attention outwards (on the rights of society at large) as well as inwards (on the rights of the self).

YOU'RE BRAVER THAN YOU BELIEVE, AND STRONGER THAN YOU SEEM, AND SMARTER THAN YOU THINK.

A. A. MILNE

DEVELOP SELF-DISCIPLINE

Self-discipline functions a bit like a muscle – it needs practice, and the more you exercise it the stronger it gets. With strong self-discipline, you can control your emotions, impulses and appetites, as well as your performance, and build the necessary discipline to manage how happy (or sad) you feel. Self-discipline is also vital to your overall happiness because many of the activities that boost your happiness (such as regular exercise) take a while to develop into a habit.

Scientists have demonstrated that self-control can have dramatic benefits in life. For instance, people with high self-control are less likely to turn to drugs, alcohol and crime, and are more likely to manage their money well and get along better with other people.

So how do you go about increasing your self-discipline? You'll need to take small steps at the start and build up from there. The key is to set the bar high enough that you have something to aim for, but not so high that you haven't got a hope of achieving it.

RESIST ME

BE APPRECIATIVE

Our ability to appreciate excellence, whether in nature or man-made, is considered to be one of the most important strengths according to research carried out in the past decade. A person who is high on this strength not only feels a sense of wonderment at what is going on around them in the natural world – such as noticing the first crocus in spring or the way the pavements seem to sparkle with frost in the winter – but also at the gifts and talents shown by people around them.

A person who is low on the strength of appreciation might see what is going on around them, but it fails to move them emotionally. Being open to beauty and excellence suggests that you are creating opportunities to feel the positive emotions of joy, pleasure and elation, whereas if you don't even take the time to notice these things, that door is well and truly closed.

BEING OPEN TO BEAUTY AND EXCELLENCE SUGGESTS THAT YOU ARE CREATING OPPORTUNITIES TO FEEL THE POSITIVE EMOTIONS OF JOY, PLEASURE AND ELATION

FIND YOUR SPIRITUALITY

Religious faith gives many people a sense of meaning and purpose in life. There are a great many other benefits associated with practising religion such as: better coping with crises; less vulnerability to depression; being more forgiving; being more hopeful and optimistic; and having more compassion.

Faith communities provide social, emotional and sometimes material support, so members may feel that they belong to a like-minded community that respects and appreciates them. Even when religion isn't practised communally, people still have a private relationship with a divine being, which makes them feel loved and cared for, as well as giving them a source of reassurance and personal strength.

Those who search for spiritual self-transcendence without believing in the existence of a God have a lot in common with religious people. Spiritual people are generally happier, have better physical and psychological health, happier marriages and live longer than those who are not.

86

PUT VALUE IN EXPERIENCES

What can we do to avoid materialism and its downfalls? Scientific evidence suggests that spending money on experiences, such as going on holiday, going out for dinner or taking up a new hobby, makes people happier than spending it on possessions.

So rather than going shopping for the latest designer fashions or gadgets, why not consider spending the same money on a holiday to visit somewhere new or an experience day at a vineyard or racecourse? Or, rather than spending money at all, look for activities and experiences that are free, such as exploring a new area of the place where you live or work, meeting new people at networking or socializing events or teaching yourself a new skill online. After all, curiosity and learning new things (see pages 39 and 64) are all beneficial to our wellbeing.

SEPARATE NEEDS AND WANTS

Although there has been a significant rise in wealth in the past 50 years in most developed countries, levels of happiness have stayed pretty much the same. According to psychologist Tim Kasser, this problem occurs because we confuse our wants and needs.

Need is only a small part of why we act the way we do. Wants, while they may seem like needs, are much more rooted in emotion; it can be easy to feel unfulfilled if we persistently perceive our desires as must-haves.

IT CAN BE EASY TO FEEL UNFULFILLED IF WE PERCEIVE OUR DESIRES AS MUST-HAVES.

Kasser says people who have materialistic values (see page 108) and who pursue goals such as wealth, possessions, celebrity and status tend to have lower life satisfaction and self-esteem and place less emphasis on relationships with other people. So, next time you feel disheartened that you can't afford or don't have access to something, question whether your feelings relate to wants or needs.

88

KEEP GROWING

Personal growth is a valuable life goal; continuing to try new things, learn new skills and further develop yourself as a person can make a difference to your happiness. Choose goals related to realizing your potential.

At work you can develop yourself in new areas, acquire new skills and volunteer for assignments, which will strengthen your self-confidence and resilience, and make it easier for to take on new roles in the future.

Personal growth and happiness

- Be open to new experiences and activities, and try new ways of doing things (see page 56).
- Value experiences that challenge how you think about yourself and the world.
- See yourself as continually growing and expanding.
- Take note of your improvement over time.
- Enjoy being in new situations, which mean you have to change your familiar ways of doing things.

WORK ON YOUR STRENGTHS

First, identify your strengths: you can complete an online assessment or use the questions below to help you get more familiar with your forte.

The next step is to find ways of using your strengths. For example, if your strength is curiosity, choose an unfamiliar dish from the restaurant menu instead of your old favourite. If it's leadership, organize a social get-together. If it's creativity, enroll in a painting or pottery class. See how many different ways you can use your strengths and observe the effect it has on your happiness levels.

How to identify your strengths

- Think about some everyday things that you enjoy doing – what do you enjoy the most and why?
- What are you doing when at your best?
- What are you doing when you feel most alive and full of energy?
- Thinking back to when you were young, what were your best times? What were you doing?
- What are you doing when you feel that you are expressing the real you?

LEARN HOW TO SAY NO

NO!

Many of us feel compelled to agree to every request in the spirit of being accommodating and gaining respect and good feeling, but this can leave us with no time for ourselves. Being too ambitious in your commitments is ultimately self-destructive, leaving you exhausted, stressed and irritable.

Establishing what your boundaries are with regard to commitments is the first step in putting yourself first. Consider both what you are reasonably able to do and what you actually enjoy doing. Sometimes it might be appropriate to consider a compromise – for example, if you would like to agree to the request, but have limited time to do so.

You can minimize potential feelings of guilt by rationalizing the situation and separating refusal from rejection. It might also help to practise saying no in front of a mirror and to be aware of potential persuasion techniques. Finally, it's important to bear in mind that you do not need a reason to say 'no'. It's enough to want some time to yourself.

MAKE TIME FOR YOURSELF

There are times when it is good to be busy – it can help keep your mind off worrying about the future or dwelling on past problems. But if you take on too much, any of the benefits of keeping busy are outweighed by the negative effects of overworking, such as additional stress, bad moods and increased chance of physical illness.

Tips to feel less overwhelmed

- Organize yourself – keep a notebook or a diary to jot down appointments, notes and reminders. Set up a filing system if you haven't got one already.
- Learn how to delegate effectively.
- Ask for support from colleagues and friends.
- Learn how to say 'no' to additional work assertively.
- Plan! Set goals (see page 99) and stick to them.
- Avoid time wasters – resist the temptation to read and respond to every email as it arrives.
- Use the phone instead of email; it's quicker and easier.
- Recharge your batteries – at lunchtime get some fresh air, or visit an art gallery (see page 66).
- Start the day by making inroads into your big projects – leave administrative tasks and chores until last.
- Don't allow your calendar to fill up with meetings – if this is a danger, ask yourself whether you can provide your input in a different way.

TREAT WORK LIKE A VOCATION

According to psychologist Amy Wrzesniewski and her colleagues, there are three distinct ways to view your job: as a paycheck, as a career of advancement, or (most beneficially) as a calling.

Pay and promotion are still important, but the primary motivator is a sense of personal fulfilment. Research indicates that those who perceive their work as a calling experience greater satisfaction both in work and outside, so this view is the most beneficial to take.

Even if you have limited choice over the job you do, it's still possible to craft your work so as to maximize happiness. Some occupations might fall more naturally into one category or the other, but you can create meaning in whatever work you do. Treat your job like a vocation by being proud of your work and incorporating a variety of tasks that you like, even if they're not a part of your basic job description.

SHARE A HUG

Who doesn't love a hug? Hugs are the signal for warmth, affection and care, and they can also be a real antidote to feelings of anxiety, social exclusion and low self-esteem, with a significant effect on physical and mental health.

While we all intuitively know the psychological benefits of a hug, several studies have shown medical patients recovering more quickly when they were exposed to increased physical contact than those who weren't.

This is because we release the hormone oxytocin when we experience the touch of another person, which generates feel-good feelings of attachment, trust and intimacy. There is a corresponding effect on our heart rate and blood pressure as the hug also acts to lower stress hormones like cortisol. Think about the last time you hugged someone – when was it? – and aim to up your hug count in the week.

AVOID CELEBRITY WORSHIP

The increasing obsession with famous people, be it supermodels, film stars or athletes, has led psychologists to name it as a medical condition: celebrity worship syndrome.

There are two avenues of thought – one that suggests that this is perfectly healthy, evolutionary behaviour, known more popularly as the survival of the fittest. The other perspective is that this is an entirely unhealthy condition whereby, because people have trouble forming lasting, trusting relationships with ordinary people, they prefer to live out their own lives through the lives of their chosen celebrity.

Other studies suggest that even 'low level' celebrity worship reflects poorer psychological wellbeing, of greater anxiety and depression. So if you find that you're spending increasing time following the lives of your favourite pop stars or actors, then it's probably wise to take a step back and consider using your time in a way that is more likely to make you happy.

FAME

SPEND TIME WITH CHILDREN

Children bring a great deal of happiness and contentment to parents' lives: ask any of your friends, family, or colleagues who have children what is the greatest source of joy in their lives and chances are they'll say 'my kids'. Research has shown that for both married and single mothers, having a child is associated with increased wellbeing and happiness. Further research suggests, however, that the overall picture is not as clear cut as that; having children affects your life in very different ways depending on whether you're male or female, married, single or cohabiting.

The experience of having a child and our associated feelings of wellbeing (or depression) may vary depending on how much we embrace our new parenting roles.

It's more likely that on a daily basis, we feel quite stressed as parents, but in the long-term, most people see having children as a positive experience that adds significant meaning to their lives.

THE SOUL IS HEALED BY BEING WITH CHILDREN
FYODOR DOSTOEVSKY

VOLUNTEER YOUR TIME

Volunteering contributes to society but also has individual benefit. Why do people voluntarily give up precious time to assist others, whether to help local school children read, protect the coral reefs in Tobago or provide emergency relief in disaster zones? The simple fact is that volunteering, in any capacity, can improve your psychological wellbeing, increase your life satisfaction and physical health and provide a buffer against stress. It has also been suggested that more is better: doing twice as much volunteering is roughly twice as good for you. In short, volunteering is a no-brainer.

BE HOPEFUL

Being hopeful is beneficial for psychological and physical health, by buffering against interfering, self-critical thoughts and negative emotions. Hopeful thinking allows you to create a mental plan which, when you focus on it, enables you to shut out interferences.

How to increase your hope

If things aren't going according to plan, it is important not to give up hope:

- Decide what your overall plan is in as much detail as you can, and what you hope to achieve by it.

- Divide your goal into smaller, more manageable sub-goals (see page 99) so that as you achieve each sub-goal you will become more hopeful that you can achieve your overall goal.

- Motivate yourself to continue – remember what you hope to achieve and how important it is to persevere.

- Tell your family and friends about your goal – they can provide moral support if your hope starts to dwindle.

- Have a plan in mind for when things go wrong so that you can take instant action; frame any obstacles you meet as challenges to be overcome.

DEVELOP YOUR MORAL COMPASS

Our needs (for food, shelter and so on) are innate and evolutionary, but our values are acquired; we learn them as we grow up – from parents, friends and society at large. The way we rank our values is what enables us to make choices every day, which can sometimes be difficult if we have too much choice (see page 47).

The important thing to consider in relation to your happiness is whether or not your actions are consistent with your values. Research suggests that people who focus on acquiring wealth and material success above other needs, such as meaningful relationships, have an overall lower satisfaction with life. What's more, studies also show that values can play a vital role in whether or not experiences are remembered as happy ones. Even if an experience makes you feel very happy in the moment, you won't recall it as a happy one at a later date unless it matches your values.

Unlike needs, though, values can (and do) change over your lifetime. Women who are very career-oriented in early adulthood, for example, can experience a rapid shift in values when they have children. So, whatever your values and whether they change over time, if you ensure you act according to them, you'll be happier in the long run.

EVEN IF AN EXPERIENCE
MAKES YOU FEEL VERY
HAPPY IN THE MOMENT,
YOU WON'T RECALL IT AS
A HAPPY ONE AT A LATER
DATE UNLESS IT MATCHES
YOUR VALUES.

FIND YOUR IKIGAI

———————

生き甲斐

Ikigai is a Japanese concept that holds your sense of purpose in life. Meaning literally 'the happiness of always being busy', it embodies the idea that people who have found the point of crossover between what they are good at, what they love, what the world needs and what they can be paid to do are more motivated and subjectively happier than those who haven't or are unsure.

Discovering your ikigai will let you find your flow (see page 22), enable you to keep things in perspective (see page 91), develop your resilience (see page 44) and prevent your life from being dictated by negative forces, like money, power and celebrity worship. In this way, your ikigai becomes the power for contentment and satisfaction in your life.

• • • • • • • • • • • • • • • • • • •

THE PURPOSE OF LIFE IS A LIFE OF PURPOSE.

ROBERT BYRNE

• • • • • • • • • • • • • • • • • • •

100

ALWAYS KEEP LEARNING

We all aspire to keep learning, whether in formal education or not, throughout our lives. It's generally acknowledged that intellectual activity is as important to a long and happy life as is remaining physically fit and active. Researchers have found that continuing to learn in later life not only provides new knowledge and promotes intellectual stimulation, it also increases satisfaction and gives pleasure as well.

Other advantages of learning include improvements in the ability to stand up and be heard and willingness to take responsibility, broadened horizons and outlook, increased personal satisfaction, meeting people and more social interaction and being better able to deal with other people. And on top of all these benefits, older students also reported being happier and having improved quality of life.

WHAT'S STOPPING YOU?

We hope this book has provided you with some insight into the origins of happiness and the everyday things that can affect it positively or negatively, as well as some practical ideas and inspiration about what you can do differently to increase your own happiness.

The main message throughout is that you don't have to leave your happiness up to chance; there are many things you can do to increase the odds of being psychologically fitter, such as investing time and energy into building relationships, acknowledging the reality behind money, fame and materialism, and being open to trying new things.

Hopefully you now understand that becoming happier actually involves some consistent effort on your part – and that while your genes may have given you a head start in the happiness stakes, you shouldn't necessarily expect to be happier no matter what happens to you in life.

Finally, you can do a lot yourself to explore new (and old!) ways of being happy. This a very topical subject – after all, most of us would like to be happier – so you'll be able to find a great deal of information about it on the internet and in bookstores. Do be aware, however, that some will make unsubstantiated claims. There are plenty of very accessible websites, books and blogs that are based on science, and that will add depth and colour to Live Happy, so don't be afraid to explore them. Just use your common sense in deciding which are reliable, or right for you.

So, having read this book, what's stopping you? Go out and live your life to its happiest.

INDEX

First published in 2019 in Great Britain, Australia and
New Zealand by Modern Books,
An imprint of Elwin Street Limited
14 Clerkenwell Green
London EC1R 0DP
www.modern-books.com

Some of the text from this book appeared in a previous
edition of *Happiness Equation* (2008)

ISBN: 978-1-911130-93-2

10 9 8 7 6 5 4 3 2 1

Layouts designed and illustrated by Karin Skånberg

Printed in China

Disclaimer: The advice, recipes and exercises in this book are intended as a personal guide to
healthy living. However, this information is not intended to provide medical advice and it should not
replace the guidance of a qualified physician or other healthcare professional. Decisions about your
health should be made by you and your healthcare provider based on the specific circumstances
of your health, risk factors, family history and other considerations. See your healthcare provider
before making major dietary changes or embarking on an exercise programme, especially if you
have existing health problems, medical conditions or chronic diseases. The author and publishers
have made every effort to ensure that the information in this book is safe and accurate, but they
cannot accept liability for any resulting injury or loss or damage to either property or person,
whether direct or consequential and howsoever arising.

The information in this study is based on thorough academic research, with information gathered
from over 100 journal articles, and informed by book-length studies, case studies, reports and
statistics. For a full list of references, please contact the publisher.